A N... ...ers

D...
ch...
ex... ...onorary Fellow
of... ...ing. Cliff Moon has spent many
years as a teacher and teacher educator specializing
in reading and has written more than 140 books for
children and teachers. He reviews regularly for
teachers' journals.

Beautiful illustrations and superb full-colour photographs
combine with engaging, easy-to-read stories to offer
a fresh approach to each subject in the series. Each
DK READER is guaranteed to capture a child's
interest while developing his or her reading skills,
general knowledge, and love of reading.

The five levels of DK READERS are aimed at
different reading abilities, enabling you to choose
the books that are exactly right for your child:

Pre-level 1: Learning to read
Level 1: Beginning to read
Level 2: Beginning to read alone
Level 3: Reading alone
Level 4: Proficient readers

The "normal" age at which a child
begins to read can be anywhere from
three to eight years old, so these levels
are only a general guideline.

No matter which level you
select, you can be sure that you
are helping your child learn to
read, then read to learn!

LONDON, NEW YORK, MUNICH,
MELBOURNE AND DELHI

Series Editor Deborah Lock
Art Editor Sadie Thomas
Production Shivani Pandey
DTP Designer Almudena Díaz
Jacket Designer Simon Oon
Photographer Andy Crawford

Reading Consultant
Cliff Moon, M.Ed.

Published in Great Britain by Dorling Kindersley Limited
80 Strand, London, WC2R 0RL

2 4 6 8 10 9 7 5 3 1

A Penguin Company

Copyright © 2004 Dorling Kindersley Limited, London

All rights reserved. No part of this publication may be reproduced,
stored in a retrieval system, or transmitted in any form or by any
means, electronic, mechanical, photocopying, recording, or otherwise,
without the prior written permission of the copyright owner.

A CIP record for this book is
available from the British Library

ISBN 1-4053-0543-6

Colour reproduction by Colourscan, Singapore
Printed and bound in China by L Rex Printing Co., Ltd.

Photographs taken at Brompton Library
with thanks to Angela Goreham and staff;
and the entrance of Victoria Library
Thanks also to all the models: Rhianna Stamps, Caroline Stamps,
Che Commerasamy Bryers from Scallywags,
Rochea Brown, Gabby Stamps, and Anil Thomas

All other images © Dorling Kindesley Limited
For further information see: www.dkimages.com

See our complete catalogue at

www.dk.com

 **READERS**

BEGINNING
1
TO READ

A Trip to the Library

Written by Deborah Lock

A Dorling Kindersley Book

Amy and her family had just
moved to a new town.
"What is there to do here?"
asked Amy.

"We can visit the local library," said Mum.

At the library, Amy met Dan,
who was her new neighbour.
"Hello, Amy," called Dan.
"I come to the library all the time.
I'll show you around."

7

At the front desk, Dan handed some books to the librarian.

librarian

"I've brought these books back," said Dan, "but please could I renew this one?"

The librarian
checked in the books
with a scanner.

scanner

She gave Dan the book
he wanted to read again.

"Where can I become a member
of the library?" asked Amy.
"At the help desk,"
said the librarian.

At the help desk, Amy and Mum gave their names and new address to another librarian.

She gave them
their own library cards.
The librarian told them
about the library.
"We are here to help," she said.

Dan and Amy went
to the children's corner.
Each shelf was filled with books.

"I like reading about animals,"
said Amy, "but where
will I find books about them?"

shelf

"Here they are," said Dan,
pointing to some shelves.
"The books about animals
are all together."

"I'll choose some books,"
said Amy.

Mum went to the adults' area.
She looked at the display
of new books.
She read the back covers
of the books to find out
what they were about.

"It's story time," said the librarian.
Dan and Amy sat on the seat
to listen to the story.

seat

It was a story about
a lion and a mouse.

"Now you can make some
animal masks," said the librarian.
Dan made
a lion mask with
an orange mane.

mask

Amy made some fluffy ears
for her mouse mask.

"I'd like to borrow the story time book," said Amy.
"Are there any copies on the shelves?"

computer

"We can search for the title
on the computer," said Dan.

There was one copy of
the story book in the library.
Amy found it and then
looked at the other
picture books.

"We can choose videos and story tapes, too," said Dan.

video

Amy found Mum looking at
the notice boards.
"I'm finding out about things to do
in the area," said Mum.

"Can I borrow these
books and tapes?"
asked Amy.
"Yes," said Mum.
"Let's go to
the exit desk."

The librarian scanned
Amy's library card and
then the books and tapes.

She stamped
the return date
on them.
"Please return them
in three weeks,"
she said.

stamp

"Thanks," said Amy.
"I'll come again soon."

Picture word list

librarian

page 8

mask

page 22

scanner

page 10

computer

page 24

shelf

page 15

video

page 27

seat

page 20

stamp

page 30